YES

GW00359856

Chiara Lubich

YES YES, NO NO

New City London

First published under the title
Sì, sì. No, no 1973
by Città Nuova, Roma

First published in Great Britain 1977
by Mariapolis Ltd.
57 Twyford Avenue, London W3 9PZ

Reprinted 1981

© 1977 New City London

Printed in Great Britain by
Biddles Ltd, Guildford, Surrey

Nihil obstat R. J. Cuming, DD
Imprimatur Ralph Brown
Westminster, 15 February 1977

ISBN 0 904287 07 6

Contents

ARACELI'S SECRET

I KEEP ARACELI'S* photo on my table: I am prompted by the inner desire to see a living mirror of someone who knew how to incarnate what ought and must be my ideal.

She is there smiling, young and beautiful, with that true beauty that knows nothing of what is worldly and affected, that is all transparentness, innocence and decision. Sweetly delicate, the grace, however, shines especially from her eyes.

In her everything spoke of life: her youth, her affection for those of her own age and those younger than herself, for whom in Madrid she unwittingly had become a leader. One young man said, after Araceli was no longer among us, that she had left just one impression, just one heritage: God.

She had organized, among other things, a

* Araceli Nunes was a Spanish focolarina who died at the age of 24 in a car crash in 1970.

girl's musical group that won applause in public theatres from thousands of people because it literally shouted out the Gospel—so much so that rowdies sprawled in their seats who had come more to make trouble than to listen, as time went by, began to sit up and found through these unambiguous words their own dignity.

The group was called R.D.A. = revolution of love.

Anyone, even if they had never been there, who heard live recordings of one of her performances, could sense something in their veins : the thrill from the impact and the victory of truth on a public which was only a little aware of the Spirit.

Araceli loved to play. Her heart and her lucid and warm intelligence were Spanish. She knew how to detach herself, when the circumstances demanded the duty of charity to others, even from those deep and so rare meditations in which conversation with God is full, so as to dress up as a toreador and improvize with a girl disguised as a bull, all the movements of a bullfight.

She contradicted with her life the conviction that young girls today cannot live without a boy-friend, without strange experiences, without seeking drugged happiness.

Even so, she was one of them, and she had already found here on earth the fullest, the deepest happiness.

At nineteen, having heard the call of God, she left parents, home and country, and she had united with other girls in order to live the Gospel completely, giving herself totally to Christ.

She was fiercely proud of this: but was also afraid that someone who had made the same choice as she had might not understand all its unfathomable worth.

She wrote, in fact: 'May we never lose the sense of having found the most beautiful vocation in the world, of having been chosen by the "most beautiful of the sons of man", of being the richest persons in the world ...' 'I feel I have nothing to envy anyone for, because I have found an ideal that is powerful, divine, challenging, revolutionary.'

Her departure from the earth was as swift as lightning. And straightaway, several people fired by her, the living expression of an ideal, declared they wanted to take her place. They included young people, and the first to make this decision was her father.

A person who knew her said that in that last year Araceli had been transformed: she had imbued her humanity with the divine and the divine had become almost natural in her, so that she was for everybody truly a sister, a mother, a friend.

The 'race', preceded by repeated training, began when she understood with new depth this truth: *that God is to be loved with all one's heart in the present moment of life.*

She made a pact with other girls, her friends, to live like this. The important thing is that she remained faithful to it.

She knew that to put such a proposal into practice meant to know how to lose not only her own bad will, but also everything beautiful, good, and holy, that she could possess in the present but which was not willed by God for her.

So it was a simple but utterly deep concept, a truth that admits no doubts, that brought Araceli to spiritual heights which we shall know only in the next life. To love God we must do his

4

will. But his will presents itself moment by moment.

It may be expressed by external circumstances, by our own duties, by some advice from wise people or from those who represent God for us. Or even by something unexpected, sorrowful or delightful, annoying or indifferent.

And it will be understood by the attentive spirit, the vigilant soul.

It's not for nothing that the Gospel speaks so often about vigilance.

And it is the Gospel itself that focuses Man on the present, not wanting him to be worried about the future, when it makes him ask for bread from the Father just for 'today', and invites him to carry 'today's' cross and says that 'each day' has troubles enough of its own. It's also the Gospel that warns: 'No one who sets his hand on the plough and then keeps looking back is fit for the kingdom of God.'

To get used to living the present well, we Christians must know how to forget the past and how not to be worried about the future.

And this is plain good sense: since the past exists no more and the future will be when it becomes present. Catherine of Siena said: 'We don't have the fatigue which is past because the time has flown: we don't have what's to come because we can't be sure of having the time.'

Great people and saints know this principle. They are used to discerning God's voice from among the various inner voices. And in this continual practice, this discernment becomes easier and easier because the voice becomes stronger, and is amplified.

At the start perhaps it is not so easy.

Then, with complete abandonment to God, we must believe in his love and perform with decision what we consider is his will, in the confidence that if it is not, he'll put us back on the right track again. And even when God's will seems quite clear, calling us to do a job that will take hours, there's always the temptation to overcome, a scruple to be driven away, some worry to be thrown into the heart of God, wandering thoughts to get away from, various desires to say no to.

Living the present is an idea and a practice that is extraordinarily rich. Living the present grafts our whole earthly life right up to now into the course of eternal life.

François de Sales says about this: 'Every moment is entrusted with an order from God and dives into eternity to fix there what we have done with it.'

Living the present is then, for us Christians who are in the world, perhaps our only chance of becoming saints. And so it's a necessity.

By enclosing ourselves in God's will for the present moment, completely attentive to his voice, shooting forward in fulfilment of his commands, we have the possibility that only monks have, of always obeying God in their superior; we are sheltered by the walls of a heavenly cloister and told by a silent and divine 'inner bell' to take up the ever new activity which is God's unique will for us.

The present then arrives with a special gift for fulfilling our own duty well, called 'actual grace'. Raissa Maritain wrote that: 'The duties of every moment hide under their obscure appearance the truth of the divine will; they are like the sacraments of the present moment.'

Pope John XXIII lived these principles: 'I must do each thing, say every prayer, carry out that rule, as if I had nothing else to do, as if the Lord had put me into the world just to do that action well, and as if my sanctification depended entirely upon its favourable result, without thinking of before and after.'

It seems, too, as if 'living the present' is the norm of our times, which often do not allow us any alternatives. The time for dreaming, for contemplating, is almost up. Today we run. Really we run too much and to avoid becoming neurotic or going mad we have to keep ourselves in the present every moment.

Dietrich Bonhoeffer's analysis of our times makes us think. 'Up to now it seemed that it was an alienable right of human life to be able to draft a plan of life from a professional or from an individual viewpoint. But things have changed. By force of circumstances we have been thrown into a situation where we must renounce "thinking for tomorrow" (Mt. 6, 34). Being compelled to give up planning for the future drives most people into an irresponsible, superficial surrender to the limitations of the moment . . . For us there remains only the narrower path, often still to be discovered, of taking each day as if it were the last, and of living with faith and a sense of responsibility as if a great future were still in store for us.'

There are also other commentators who point out that even today people make the old mistake of dwelling on a past or on a future that does not exist and neglect the present, the only opportunity for really 'living'.

'By a strange alienation,' says the Orthodox theologian Evdokimov, 'the man of this world lives in the past, in his memories, or he awaits his future; as regards the present moment, he attempts to avoid it, and exercises his ingenuity over the best ways of "killing time". This man does not live in the here and now but in day-dreams of which he is not conscious. The ascetical saying points out: "The hour you are living, the job you are doing, the person you are meeting at this moment are the most important in your whole life." They are so important because the past and the future are non-existent abstractions without any access to eternity, which converge only on the present moment and gives itself only to those who put themselves completely into that moment. It is only in these instants that it can be reached and lived in the image of the eternal now.'

This is what Araceli did. She lived the present through love and got to her finishing line in a hurry.

This is why the words on her gravestone, which sum up her life, are the words God could have said to her: 'Come quickly, my friend, my beautiful one.'

TO BE

I HAVE HAD the opportunity of getting to know something about Vinoba Bhave, the Indian who, basing himself on the word of Christ, 'Love your neighbour as yourself', has succeeded in founding and spreading a movement among tens of millions of people in India, who share out their land.

But more than this fact, which in itself is wonderful and astonishing, there is the impact of the man himself.

He reminded me so much of Patriarch Athenagoras, the Oecumenical Patriarch.

Vinoba is right to say: what matters is 'to be'. 'To be' means for him 'to be God' – by participation that is. And Vinoba must be full of God when so many people run to see him, eager to observe a living holiness that is difficult to deny.

The way he stands, the way he moves, the simplest and most minute acts, his silence – say as much as his words. The faces surrounding him express an inner silent joy, a reflection of the spiritual richness that he possesses. I have seen the same joy on the faces of people around Athenagoras, who often come from his study moved to tears.

Vinoba and Athenagoras are both very close to men, to each man, yet it takes only a moment to realize that they already live beyond this world. And these are not just words.

This 'to be' is what most attracts every Christian who has the adventure of meeting men of this calibre. And such an experience irresistably leads us to imitate so great a reality. This is why whoever knows the way of holiness passionately turns again to the asceticism it requires – to live in God in the present moment of life. In this way we are completely separated from everything that is not God and immersed in God wherever he is present. Then our life is no longer 'existing', but fully 'being', because God, he who is, *is* in it.

And this is the life that suits the Christian, the real son of God.

What happens then is that living is a continual word, ever teaching, even if immersed in deepest silence. It could be said that when we speak of God we simply speak, but when we live like this, even if we do not speak, we shout about him.

Vinoba is right, when he emphasizes *the action of inaction*. His formula, M2A, two meditations to one action, is beautiful. We can translate it as MA, meditation and action the whole day, whether we speak or whether we are silent.

The remarkable thing is that we are describing two personalities of the present-day world which is ruled over by the myth of activism.

This gives us a lot of hope.

CATHERINE OF SIENA, CHURCH-SOUL

THE CALENDAR FOR April presents again to all Christians the great figure of the saint who was proclaimed a Doctor of the Church by Pope Paul VI a few years ago: Catherine of Siena.

But what is so special about this woman who, despite the passing of centuries, lives more than ever in the Christian consciousness and is rediscovered by each period as she who always has a word to say, a fascination that attracts, a supernatural beauty that charms and especially such a relevant and modern spirit?

How is it that so very many Christians live or eke out their Christianity leaving little or no trace behind them, while in the case of *this* Christian, the more time goes by, the more the Church honours her and the Church's children are delighted by this?

It would take volumes to answer this adequately, to cite the countless wonderful graces, miracles and wisdom that fill up her extraordinary life.

Yet I believe one single word can answer this: the fact is that Catherine is a *Church-soul*.

Now just as the Church will never pass away and, notwithstanding the unavoidable struggles which must characterize it will never see the sun set, so Catherine, having become one with the Church, has, one may say, a like destiny.

It's through this, her 'being Church', that Catherine still has something to say to all of us Christians today, intent in thousands of ways and as much as we can, on understanding, on loving, on bringing a lacerated Christianity together again into the one and only Church which is *her very own* word.

Catherine is a creature in whose heart charity burns so strongly, that it is like Christ's, with a love that becomes a true, holy passion for the Church.

Let's look at her in action.

Although she inspired a religious current, the 'Catherinites', who followed her spirituality which is summed up in the two words, 'fire' and 'blood', this is not her chief work, but rather her chief work is her untiring effort to bring the Pope back to Rome. Quite clearly here she is

15

facing the problems of the Church with complete openness.

If her apostolate is analysed, we are struck by the same impression. At a certain moment, Catherine passes from a private to a public level. The immediate reason for this was the fact that among her followers there were also noted personalities from the political as well as from the religious field. And she saw them all not through the distorting lens of restricting interests, even though religious ones, but in terms of their complete personality.

If Catherine has something to do with a Cardinal, for example, she considers him in the context of the influence he has in the Church. If she has dealings with a prince, she also follows him in his political action. He is a follower of hers, but Catherine loves him for the Church, for mankind.

She shares with all her children their struggles, their anxieties, everything they are living through.

And if she maintains a prolific correspondence, not only with men and women in the humblest circumstances, but also with the Church and state authorities, if she interests herself in news of current affairs, this is because her openness has the measure of the Church and of mankind.

Then if we hear her pray, we have not the slightest doubt that she has only one great love. Her desires and her requests to God are for the Church: 'Oh eternal God, receive the sacrifice of my life in this mystical body of the holy Church. I have nothing to give other than what you have given me. Take my heart then and squeeze it out on the face of this Spouse.'

Catherine has no peace till the Church finds unity again around the Pope. She lives and loves the Church so passionately that her every move is inspired by this flame.

Nor is the doctrinal side secondary in the virgin of Siena if she has been proclaimed a Doctor on account of her wisdom.

Catherine writes books that Jesus himself dictates. And yet she is grateful to Brother Raymond for what he does for her with his doctrine. He guarantees that she remains faithful to the teaching of the Church.

Catherine acts like the true reformers. They submit their illuminations or revelations to those who can tell them the thought of the Church, and let themselves be guided by those for whom they themselves are at times, in another way, the guide.

The false reformers, on the contrary, stigmatize error with cold judgement and separate themselves.

Catherine is not scandalized and does not withdraw in the face of the disconcerting deviations of the Church at that time, and she always finds a way of living her 'being Church'.

When, for example, she herself seems to be an object of discontent to the Pope at that time, she exploits that very situation to lodge herself even further within the heart of the mystical body, and writes to the pontiff like this: 'Most Holy Father . . . if you are displeased and are indignant towards me, if you abandon me, I shall hide myself in the wounds of the crucified Christ, whose vicar you are; and I know that he will receive me since he does not will the death of a sinner. And since I am received by him, you will not chase me away,' so Catherine concludes, still together, 'we will stand in the front line to fight dauntlessly for the sweet Spouse of Christ.'

Catherine, just when she feels weakest, considers herself most Church and makes her weakness its glory, and completely forgetting herself, she sees nothing else and loves nothing but the interests of the Spouse of Christ.

Because the fire of Christ is burning in her heart, she experiences strongly the sense of the Church as a family.

She has a spiritual family herself and, of course, lives for them. She goes out of her way so much for them that Brother Raymond can confess: 'All of us because of this, call the virgin "mamma", because she really was our "mamma", giving birth to us day by day from the womb of her mind, until we became copies of Christ.'

But at the same time, Catherine's family is the entire Church. She is so taken up with love for it that she can with amazing directness assume the authority of a mother, often cutting short the intricate controversies of the Church by stating her determination with a peremptory formula: 'It is God's will and mine.'

Somebody might ascribe her behaviour to the following reason: Catherine speaks like this because her will coincides by now with God's will.

Yes, her will coincides with that of God, but

it is also her own because she is Church and shares in some measure in the motherhood of the Church for all.

In the forcefulness with which she affirms her own will, we do not feel a juridicial authority, which Catherine does not have, but that maternal authority which has given everything to keep God's family united together: an authority similar to Mary's.

Not only is the Church her family, it is her home, her city.

Without doubt, everything that tears apart the net of relationships of peace which should make the Church the city of light for the world, tears apart her own inner being.

It's enough to think of certain painful moments in the last years of her life.

The Pope had returned to Rome at last, but in the meantime an anti-pope had been elected who had his see at Avignon, and many cardinals had sided with him.

Catherine then went through the darkest night of her whole existence: perhaps she felt herself responsible for that schism, through having persuaded the legitimate Pope to leave Avignon for Rome?

But look at her, as though desiring to concentrate in herself that entire trauma of the mystical body, as though desiring to suffer at the centre of this pain, making her way to St Peter's, where she feels nearer the Pope, to pray there the whole day long for unity and peace to return. And this is what she writes to Brother Raymond: 'When it is still dawn you may see a dead woman going to St Peter's . . . There I stay like that almost till the hour of vespers; and I would not wish to leave that place day or night until I see this people quietened a little and settled down with their father.'

This is significant: Catherine feels the need to make her way even physically to the centre of Christianity making St Peter's her church.

Church-soul, Catherine teaches us that the Church is itself if it is *one* in faith and in love.

For lots of well known reasons, today too, we need to learn from such a great teacher and our hearts will be inflamed by her ardent passion and we can all effectively serve our Mother Church wherever we are on earth, whether the position of responsibility we hold is big or small.

NO ONE HAS THOUGHT SO MUCH
OF MAN

JESUS HAS DIED for us.
That means Jesus has died for me:
God has died for me.
This is the greatness of Man; that a God should
have died for him.
We can talk about humanism and let us give it
the whole Christian dimension: no one will ever
attain this peak.
No one has ever considered Man so great as to
think that God has loved him and has loved him
right to the point of dying for him.
But rather than thinking of Christian humanism,
I like to think that Jesus, God, has died for
me.
It is impossible not to be happy,
Not to enjoy life in him,
Not to offer him our pains.
If Jesus has died for me,
He is always thinking of me,

He loves me always.
And I?
I should always think of him,
I should love him always.

IT IS LOVE THAT COUNTS

SPEAKING OF LOVE, of charity, Pope Paul VI
in an address to the Australian bishops gathered
together in Sydney, said: 'This is – it seems to
us – the principle virtue required of the Catholic
Church at this hour in the world.'

If this is so, as indeed it is, the twentieth
century Christian has to be 'living charity'
moment by moment, to answer the needs of the
Church and the questions of the world.

This is what the Christian should aim at:
true love, knowing well how everything counts
if it is inspired and carried out by love, and
nothing counts without it, at least in the final
reckoning of his own life.

This then is what the Christian should commit himself to, so that he can say after finishing
every task: *this is a work that will remain.*

It should be like this in his everyday work,
in his reading, in attending to his own affairs,
in the education of his children, in his conversa-

tion, his travels, the way he dresses, his manner of eating, even his sleep. In his littlest action . . . with all the unexpected things God will ask of him day by day.

So it should be, and this is extremely consoling, in the case of the person who is sick and confined to bed or incapacitated by an endless convalescence and can do practically nothing.

Like this, just like this – how often have we said it, how often forgotten it – because it is not the job, the writing, the activity, even if it is apostolic, that counts, but love that should be the soul of our life.

And everyone can do this.

For God, every action in itself is indifferent. It is the love that counts. It is love that keeps the world going, since if a person even has a mission to carry out, this is all the more fruitful the more it is soaked in love.

But we should remember that there is love and love. And the love distilled from a shred of life that is wearing itself out like Christ on the cross, is surely more powerful than the love of one who offers – and everything is to be offered – the joyful and serene things life gives him.

Then, so that we Christians be not behind the times, we must try to put love into everything we do, especially making sure we do not lack love when life proves most difficult and painful.

THAT WAS HOW I FOUND YOU

WHEN THEY SPEAK of love, Lord, perhaps men think of something that is always the same.

But how varied love is!

I remember that when I met you I didn't worry about loving you. Perhaps because it was you who met me and you thought that you yourself would fill my heart. I remember that sometimes I was all flame, even if the burden of my humanity was bothering me and I felt as if I was dragging a load. Then, even then, by your grace, I understood a little who I was and who you were, and I saw that flame as a gift of yours.

Then you showed me a way of finding you. 'Under the cross, under every cross – you told me – there am I. Embrace it and you will find me.'

You told me this many times and I don't remember the arguments you used. I know that you convinced me.

Then, as each suffering arrived, I thought of you and with my will I gave you my yes ... But the cross stayed: the darkness that blacked out the soul, the torment that tore it to pieces, or whatever ... all the crosses of life.

But you, later on, taught me to love you in my brothers and then, having met sorrow I did not stop there, but accepting it, I concerned myself about the person who stood beside me, forgetting about myself. And after a few seconds, returning to myself, I found my sorrow had disappeared.

So for years and years, there was the continual gymnastic of the cross, and the asceticism of love. I passed through many trials and you know this: you who count the hairs of my head, you have counted them in your heart.

Now love is different, it is not only will.

I knew that God is Love, but I did not believe it in this way.

TOWARDS A NEW HUMANISM

TODAY, IN THE consumer society, there is just one thing that people want to save: time. If we take a look at the advertisements, if we listen to the radio, or follow the television, words like 'quick', 'here', 'fast', 'right away', 'in two minutes' ... keep coming up.

Even sculpture and painting use few strokes and poor materials, but above all they operate in a hurry, although in past centuries art demanded time, a lot of time ...

One year we cross a stretch of open ground, an uncultivated meadow on the outskirts of the city. Next year we pass by again and admire a display of houses, of huge apartment blocks.

Roads which have been used for decades vanish in a few months without our noticing it, and in their place we find magnificent motorways ...

Everything is done at high speed and many things are prefabricated.

29

Not to speak of communications which bring even persons who live furthest away from us closer, saving days of travel.

Even those open to the deepest things, even sensitive Christians drawn by inexpressible mysteries, cannot help feeling the influence of this new rhythm to which humanity is advancing, especially in the most developed countries.

For most people hours spent in solitary contemplation, in prolonged meditation, seem anachronistic.

People prefer to find short but sure formulas for reaching the goal, which in this case is nothing less than union with God.

It is in this context that a phrase attributed to St Bonaventure which has been certainly proved by experience, seems to me to be particularly relevant. In it he affirms that a person will go farther on the way to God in forty days *if he never stops*, than another in forty years (even if he is enclosed in a monastery with every help to be perfect), who stops every now and then 'in the vale of imperfections and venial sins.'

An affirmation like this is bound to strike us,

it cannot but electrify each one of us with a charge of enthusiasm.

It cannot but make us put the question : how can we manage not to stop in imperfections and in venial sins?

The answer seems obvious : by constantly seeking perfection.

But what does perfection consist of?

We know that from Christ : it consists of *love*, because whoever loves does not sin; it consists of love for God, which finds its concrete expression in love for our neighbour.

It is with charity to our brothers that we pass continually from death to life, and remain in that life which is the guarantee of the life that will have no end.

Today, when the whole world is going forward towards a newly-minted humanism which finds the most varied nuances in the different ideologies, and which entrances the masses as well as individuals, the Christian imperative of charity seems extremely relevant : this is a humanism where man looks at man, and one people looks at another people *through the transfiguring lens of the person of Christ.*

The Second Vatican Council has become

aware of the new place that man is taking in the concept of modern society. It reaffirms that 'the fundamental law of human perfection, and so also of the transformation of the world, is the new commandment of charity. Those, therefore, who believe in divine charity are given the certainty by Christ that the way of charity is open to all men and that the efforts aimed at realizing charity are not in vain.'

Pope Paul VI, commenting on this passage, has said: 'The Church tends to confirm man, to respect him, to make him conscious of his greatness. She does not humiliate him but exalts him, she does not drug him but wakes him up to the sense of his own dignity. She never despises him – and how could she? – but esteems him and loves him, bends towards him, embraces him and donates to him, as it were, her own heart, like Jesus who washed the feet of the apostles, like the saints who knew how to embrace the lepers and the sick. Charity shiningly plays the role which the Church is called to, the role of bringing man to his full development.'

The saints were always right in this matter. They reached the height of perfection because they loved their neighbour.

It is said of Catherine of Siena: '... but Catherine used to think that it was not enough to give just what we were asked for, that it was not enough not to turn a deaf ear to those who were begging from us. So she began to seek out the needy. While everyone was asleep she used to go out and leave bread, a flask of wine and a sack of flour, or a basket of eggs on their door-steps. And then she slipped away quietly without anyone noticing her ...'

Teresa of Avila, a great contemplative, also affirmed: 'The Lord wants works. For example, he wants you not to worry about missing that hour of devotion, in order to console a sick person to whom you can bring comfort by making his suffering your own, fasting yourself, if necessary, to give him something to eat. This is what true union with the will of God means!'

And men who are very close to Christianity cannot have a different view. How beautiful is Ghandi's affirmation in his book *Ancient as the Mountains*: 'If we love those who love us, this is not non-violence. Non-violence is loving those who hate us. I know how difficult it is to follow this sublime law of love. But aren't all great and good things difficult? Love for one's enemy is the most difficult of all. But with the grace of God even this most difficult thing becomes easy to do if we want it . . .'

'The golden rule is to be friends of the world and to consider the whole human family as one. Whoever distinguishes between the faithful of his own religion and those of another, misleads the members of his own religion and opens the way to rejection and irreligion.'

If today even the thought of those who do not believe in God penetrates young and often inexperienced people deeply, it is because it presents a certain love towards men.

The words of Pope Paul VI's encyclical letter *The Progress of Peoples* certainly apply to these people: humanism, yes, he agrees 'but open to the Absolute'. Otherwise the Apostle would warn: 'It is worth nothing'.

Very helpfully, Pope Paul VI points out that the precept of Christian charity contains in itself potentials for development that no philanthropy, no sociology, can ever equal. And examining our charity, he continues: 'Charity is still contracted and shut in by the confines of customs, of interests, of egoisms which should, we believe, be opened out.'

It becomes logical then to draw a conculsion: there is an urgent need *to transform all our relationships* with brothers, parents, relatives, colleagues, acquaintances, with all the inhabitants of the world, into Christian relationships.

And impelled and illuminated by love, to initiate works for individuals and groups, remembering that if a cup of water will receive its reward, then a hospital, a school, an orphanage, a remedial institute and so on, when built and run as a means of expressing our charity, will prepare us for a brilliant final examination of life.

God, indeed, will ask us:

'I was hungry in your husband, in your children, in the same way as I was in the peoples of India, and you, seeing me in them, have given me to eat.'

'I was thirsty, I was naked in your little ones every morning, just as I was in your brothers of many nations where the conditions of life are inhuman, and you, seeing me always in everyone, have clothed me with what you had.'

'I was an orphan, famished, sick, in the baby in your district, just as I was in the people of Pakistan, overwhelmed by disasters, and you have made every effort to assist me.'

'You have put up with your mother-in-law or with a nervous wife, just as you did with your threatening workers or with your employer still as lacking in understanding as ever, because you were convinced that perfect social justice will only flower from social charity. And you have done this because you have seen me in everyone.'

'You have visited a relative in prison, you have prayed and brought possible relief to those who live under oppression and who are "violated in their most inner spirit".'

Then we, amazed, will let out from our lips only one phrase: thank you. Thank you, my God, for having opened for us on earth a way, the straightest and the shortest way for reaching our heavenly destination quickly and directly.

IF ONE FINE morning a man woke up, and if to his surprise and then growing interest, he were to discover that the world around him had been transfigured and that he was seeing everything with new eyes, it would be a beautiful day for him.

An unseen person has filled with himself, with his more than human fragrance, the atmosphere that surrounds the man.

The faces of well-known friends, of the poor beggarman at the street corner, of the workers that sweat beside him all day long, of the granddaughter gravely ill, of the grandfather already old, the faces of his sons and daughters, of his wife ... are no longer as they were before: an exceptional light has made their features and movements radiant with beauty, and a high nobility shines out from each one of them.

The man notices in the air a warm, fatherly voice he can barely hear, yet it expresses love:

love that is true, sincere, personal love for him, for him who has so often felt passed over, cheap, useless, solitary: an atom of a vast society that pulverizes him to anonymity.

The voice speaks to him both firmly and gently: look, now do this, now do that. And although he used to be wilful and rebellious, now he can't resist such attractive commands and he follows every call.

He doesn't even know himself anymore. He used to be lazy, bored, always tired out, but a new youthfulness has penetrated his veins, and now, fast and agile, he completes even the toughest assignments.

The bells that are ringing, the radio that informs him, the gifts that arrive, the article he is reading, even the bad news he is told by the neighbours in the street, everything that surrounds him takes on a new meaning. Particular things, even the most insignificant, open his mind to broad visions of life, the deep meanings of history. In the chaos of everyday events he begins to catch hold of a thread that seems to tie everything together, to rearrange, even to bring them into harmony, and somehow lead everything to a good and higher end.

And so bright is the light that illuminates his mind, so strong the thrust of love in his will, that he is not satisfied till he communicates to others what he is living and experiencing: so that he can see with them, feel with them, share with them the joy that has opened out his heart.

His day will end in a sunset that will seem to him like dawn and he will see the new day arriving like a further sequence in an inconceivably extraordinary film, whose plot he knows only partly, because the whole is known perfectly and guided by an Other.

And he is joyfully waiting to know, to follow this divine adventure that has now begun for his life, if only he no longer closes his ear to that voice, if only he will keep his heart, changed from stone to flesh, for loving him who loves him and for carrying out all that pleases him.

This transformation, this transfiguration of men and of the world is not a mere dream, sheer fantasy. This experience is by no means rare in the life of a Christian who one fine day understands that if God is love and he is the object of this love, he cannot but abandon himself trustingly in God.

It is the moment in which his life changes

course and disappointed with the effort of creating a destiny for himself on his own, which never fully satisfies him, he decides to adapt himself to the plan God has thought out for him. He remembers he possesses a great gift: freedom, and recognizes that nothing can be more reasonable for a creature, a child of God, than the act of freely submitting his freedom to him who gave it to him.

So he proposes, from that moment, to do not his own but God's will.

This is the great discovery, the wise decision that true Christians have made.

Thérèse of Lisieux said: 'I am only afraid of one thing: doing my own will.'

And good Pope John XXIII wrote: 'My true greatness consists in doing completely and with perfection, the will of God.'

Catherine of Siena, who knew from experience the effects produced in the soul of those who joyfully do God's will, exclaimed: 'Oh sweetest will, who gives life and takes death away, grant light and consume the darkness!'

And John of the Cross, referring to those who live in depth the Christian experience states: 'There no longer exist two wills but only one,

God's, which is also the will of the soul,' and he explains: 'The will of the soul changed into that of God does not get lost but becomes entirely the will of God ...'

This attitude of desiring to fulfill God's will and not one's own is, above all, the only and perfect way of behaving that *all* Christians should follow.

God, in fact, says through Isaiah that a new name will be conferred on the Church: 'My will in her;' and François de Sales comments: 'It is as if God said that the non-Christians each have in their heart their own will, but all the true sons of the Saviour will leave their own will aside; nor will there be more than a single will ... a universal ruler and Lord to give life to, and to govern and direct all souls ...'

This true life of the Christian transfers him to a higher region where greatness, nobility and the atmosphere of paradise reign, radically changing his often flat and colourless existence, as has been clearly taught by Pope Paul VI:

'The great plans of God, the providential enterprises that the Lord has in mind for human destinies, can co-exist with and make themselves at home with the most ordinary conditions of life.'

'We know that to make our capricious will coincide with the willing of God is the secret of the *great life*. It is the grafting of ourselves onto the Lord's thoughts and the entering into his all-seeing plans, into his mercy and his magnanimity.'

'Each person should be so attentive to the voices of Heaven as to pose himself the question: What is God's will in my existence?'

'No life is banal ... we are fore-ordained for something great, for God's Kingdom, for his invitations, for conversation with him, for living with and being drawn up to him ...'

Each of the various ideologies which animate present-day society, has its own vision of the world that is decked out as attractively as possible to win over individuals and the masses. With these ideologies one lives always with the hope of a better future.

In order that the various ways of interpreting

mankind, its history and its destiny may not deceive, even in good faith, those who dwell on our planet, it is necessary that we Christians should put forward again, in the most genuine manner, and in the most varied and faraway parts of the earth in which we are present, the Gospel message. And we'll have to do this with such involvement and such conviction that it can be said again of us twenty centuries later: what the soul is for the body, the Christians are for the world.

Today, also, when individuals and groups sometimes drive themselves crazy in search of a life different from the one they are living; when money and prosperity have shown themselves unable to satisfy the human spirit and people turn to frenzied diversions, to erotic folly, to drugs for experience of a new hallucinatory vision of life, it is absolutely necessary that we put forward again the true Christian vision of life.

What drives our unfortunate brothers on is not all evil: they are driven on by the thirst for happiness, without which man would not be man.

So then, the fullness of joy is the fruit of Christianity when it is lived as Christ has taught it: joy even in sorrow, joy that flowers from suffering, from sacrificing one's self, one's own views, one's own personal will, one's own ego, so as to leave room for God, for his plans, for his wise and radiant plans for the world and for each one of us.

THE ESSENTIAL FOR TODAY

THE HIPPIES, EVEN in their own extravagant ways have adopted a remark of Robert Kennedy's as their own: 'The tragedy of American youth is that they have everything except for one thing. And this one thing is the essential.'

From these words, as from others by Ghandi, Buddha, etc., the hippies get inspiration for their original way of life and for an elementary philosophy which, even if it destroys objective values, still sounds like a reprimand to the society which produced them, almost like the unwelcome voice of its conscience.

Basically, the attitude of these 'flower people' – even if expressed with different nuances, and in less regrettable attitudes and with more noble intentions – is that of the majority of young people today, who protest because unconsciously they sense the absence of what is essential for the life of man.

If it is true that the Spirit of the Lord blows powerfully on Christians of the most varied denominations to bring them back to the unity of the Church of Christ, it is no less true that the whole of humanity, whether believing or not, is enveloped in an atmosphere which is certainly not the work of man or the effect of his civilization, but has very different origins.

This atmosphere, which now only a few people are unaware of and which no one can withdraw from, is a deep sense of *universal brotherhood* which is taking root in mankind more and more, even through the frequent sorrowful events that seem to prove the exact opposite.

Paul's words could be a slogan for our times, especially for young people: 'There is neither Greek nor Jew, neither slave nor free.'

This deep awareness allows us to have experiences today which, a few years ago, were regarded as unthinkable and impossible.

Whoever, for example, has had the chance, through the closest brotherhood in Christ, to witness to his own Christian faith in a purely Islamic environment, becomes aware that Muslims are attracted by one truth: that God is not only great, powerful, all-knowing, the Living, the Everlasting, the Real, the Light, but he is *Love*: he is the Father of all.

The same happens even among pagans who, up till yesterday, had lived in idolatry or animism, when they come into contact with authentic Christians. It is impressive to see that nothing interests these brothers of ours so much as the discovery of God as charity, a father who loves everyone as his children.

While the non-Christian part of humanity is getting closer today to an understanding of who God truly is, Christians are making a wonderful *rediscovery* of him.

When Pope Paul gave his commentary on the Creed, he made two affirmations that found a special echo in our hearts and gave ancient truths a new resonance.

He defined God as: 'He is Who is and he is Love,' and among the characteristics of Christ he recalled that 'He has given us his new commandment, to love one another as he has loved us.'

47

Before the Council, although these truths had always existed, it was clear to the people above all that God is he who is, and that Jesus has saved us.

Now the word *love*, which denotes the essence of God, and the *commandment of love* which sums up Christ's desires, further clarify these pivots of our faith.

Not only that, but this more explicit definition of who God is, and the Christian people's resulting faith in this definition could be the *keynote* for the beginning of a general renewal in the life of the Church.

It is one thing in fact to know we can turn to a Being who exists, who has pity on us, who has paid for our sins. It is another thing to live and feel ourselves at the centre of the special love of God, with the resulting banishment of every fear that holds us back, and of every loneliness, every sense of being orphaned, every uncertainty.

When a girl knows she is loved, life changes for her: everything around her seems more beautiful and every detail takes on value. She herself is inclined to be better and kinder to others.

Infinitely stronger is the experience of a Christian when he acquires a deeper understanding of the truth that *God is love.*

Then the boring everyday life brightens up, a tragic life is made sweet, a dramatic existence peacefully calms down, and we're prepared to change our own limited programmes to fit in with others planned in heaven.

Such a person knows he is loved and believes with his whole being in this love. He abandons himself to it confidently and wishes to follow it.

Whether the circumstances of life are sad or joyful, they are lit up because there is a reason which is love behind them, and love has willed or permitted them all to happen.

Beneath every fact, every circumstance, every meeting, every duty, there is the will of One who certainly loves without deceit and who orders everything for good.

The creature who was weak and hesitant before, begins to have a relationship with the creator which gives him confidence and makes him strong, understanding and loving.

Soon after this revelation and the declaration

of love made by its God, the soul cannot resist declaring its own love to God.

And so begins the ascent towards the goal we are all called to: to be perfect Christians, to be saints.

God's love, belief in his love, to love in answer to his love, these are the absolute musts of today.

They constitute the essential thing the present generation is waiting for. Without them the world is in danger of running off the rails.

To discover, or rather, to rediscover that God is love is modern man's greatest adventure.

In the encyclical letter *Ecclesiasm Suam* Pope Paul VI affirms:

'We are convinced that love should take today the place that belongs to it, the first, the highest in the scale of religious and moral values, and not just in theory but in the practice of the Christian life. This applies not only to love for God ... but also to the love which as a reflection of our love for God we should pour out on ... the human race. Love explains everything. Love inspires everything. Love makes everything possible. Love renews

everything . . .'
And which of us doesn't know this?

And if we do know it, isn't this perhaps the hour of love?

THE GREAT GAINS

THE FACT THAT Jesus brought love on earth does not mean that he did not express the entire force of God's wrath towards those who exploit his goodness, or are not willing to accept the obvious truth, or who do not keep the promises they have made.

I was deeply impressed by one of his parables. It begins like this: 'I am the true vine, and my Father is the vinedresser. Every branch in me that bears no fruit he *cuts away*, and every branch that does bear fruit he *prunes*, to make it bear more fruit.'

And I was terrified by that 'he cuts away'.

This is no joking matter. Because God, precisely because he is love, is also just. His parables in the New Testament are full of teachings on justice. So that the best we Christians should expect is that God will 'prune' us. Only in this way can we have confirmation that we have loved him.

On the other hand, whether we correspond to his grace or we obstruct or despise it, in this life we will meet suffering.

God either cuts away or prunes.

There are people today who do not take the difficulties of life as trials sent by God. Among Christians there is a wide-spread sense of repulsion, a grumpiness, a desire to have a break from the effort of loving God and one's neighbour. This state of mind is often provoked by a dubious protest which distorts the true meaning of suffering, and contaminates even practising Christians.

The truth is that as long as we are grafted onto the vine, we ought rather to *welcome* the farmer's pruning.

We are united to the vine if God's grace is in us. And the best way to prevent its loss is to nourish this divine life, constantly exploiting moment by moment that *particular* help which God always gives so that we can act according to his will in every moment, in every circumstance of our existence.

It follows that to live like this, we must deny

our will when it is not in harmony with God's will.

In this way we ourselves will prune our worst self in order to let Christ, our best self, live in us.

The words of the Gospel passage which follows in fact say: 'Abide in me and I will remain in you.'

Then Jesus adds: 'I am the vine and you are the branches: he who abides in me and I in him bears much fruit, for apart from me you can do nothing.'

Here then is the first effect of the life of grace we bear: *much fruit*.

The spiritual fruitfulness of a Christian, of a community of Christians, of a Christian movement, is proportionate to the interior life of its members, to the extent that they, the branches, are united to the vine.

Further on we read: 'Anyone who does not abide in me is thrown away as a branch and withers. The withered branches are heaped together, thrown on the fire and burnt.'

And here the fear and perhaps terror returns for anyone of us who might want to resist grace,

54

because we do not know where the descent may lead.

Even someone who thinks 'I've made it', *must remember* the saying that 'the corruption of the best is the worst.'

The second great gain to be had by remaining in Jesus is we *obtain*: 'If you abide in me and my words abide in you, ask whatever you will, and it shall be done for you.'

How often are our hearts full of worries! Someone is suffering and we can do nothing for him; someone far away has lost a relative and it is not possible to be beside him; there is a disappointment to be consoled, an activity we long to support, a situation in the balance ... and we feel everything weighing on our poor shoulders.

And then? This is the solution: to ask and to obtain.

But we obtain if we remain in him. And we obtain all, we obtain an infinity of things from him, while we can dedicate ourselves to only one thing.

A third consequence of this way of living is:

we give glory to God.

This is one of the yearnings that the Holy Spirit often puts in the hearts of faithful Christians, and it is one of the greatest and most common aspirations of the saints. In fact, the Gospel goes on: 'In this will my Father will be glorified: that you may bear fruit ...'

Jesus, having openly declared his love that calls for love, ends with another promise: 'I have said these things to you so that my joy may be in you and *that your joy may be complete.*'

To bear fruit, to obtain graces, to give glory to God, to have the fullness of joy, are the great, precious, divine gains God reserves for those who remain united to his Son.

WHEN SOMEONE PASSES BY US

WHEN SOMEONE PASSES by us during the day, at work or at school, our only task is to always love.

But we must love *as Jesus.*

To do this, we must always listen to his voice speaking within us, so that we do not make mistakes by exaggeration or by default.

The Gospel warns us, for example, not to give holy things to dogs, and even though we can and should always consider ourselves inferior to everyone else, since God alone knows the graces he has given us and which we have not made enough use of, we must be very careful not to speak of 'holy things' in surroundings which have not been prepared to receive them.

Otherwise they will be despised, 'trampled on', and we will be ridiculed, 'torn to pieces', as the Gospel puts it.

At the same time, we must remember that the

Gospel itself also teaches us to love our neighbour *as ourselves* and, therefore, to share the spiritual goods we may have, the light which God gives us, with whoever is disposed to receive them.

In the first case, we must bear witness to Jesus only with our life. In the second case, we must also bear witness with words.

Christians who seek to present the life of the Gospel from an adventurous, poetic or romantic angle, trying to attract people with a pseudo Gospel message which flatters self-love, gives people a sense of being entrusted with an apparent mission, and gets their imagination working, can err by exaggeration.

We must not take from the life of the Gospel what is its greatest beauty: the normality of a limpid, harmonious, supernatural life which is not artificial or exaggerated, but is simple, like nature.

Nothing is known of the activities of Mary, the mother of the Creator and of all creatures among her contemporaries who were also her children. She only did the will of God: she loved Jesus and helped the apostles. And I believe that no one has lived the Gospel better than her.

Christians who are tied up too much in their own duties, who see the will of God only in them, and who close themselves in the meantime to what he expresses through circumstances, can err by default. Those people who err by default end up, for example, not loving whoever passes them by. They live in little intimacy with God, because they do not listen to his voice in each present moment of the day. Although believing themselves rightly attached to their own better duties, they are, in fact, also attached to themselves. They do not know the poetry of the Gospel, its divine adventure, because they do not know how to see the golden thread of the plan made by God's provident hand, which illuminates and designs the life of every man, including the lives of the simplest and most unknown men.

Those who sin by exaggerating sometimes appear to be over-excited, while those who sin by default are boring and gloomy. Their presence says nothing and drives people away.

The true Christian is he in whom Jesus lives always: everyone draws near to him in love and awe, because from him, as from Jesus, love and truth shine out: he is the light of the world.

UNDERDEVELOPED CHRISTIANS

THERE IS A lot said about the Third World, and action is taken as well. Yet hunger, lack of clothes and of housing, illiteracy, diseases and often the resulting immorality, still claim their victims in staggering proportions in many countries of the world.

Modern means of communication have exposed these unfortunate wounds and we have all been shaken by them more or less deeply.

Pope Paul VI's encyclical letter *The Progress of Peoples* has been a clarion call, the voice of Christ in the twentieth century, giving encouragement to organizations, groups and individuals already involved in helping peoples on the way of development, and it invited the world to do more, much more : to commit itself to that very progress which today is synonymous with peace.

In fact, much is being done and much will be done.

But unfortunately, the results we hope for do not always turn out to be proportionate to the tremendous expenditure of energy and means. And this can be shown in a thousand ways.

It is the proof of the words 'Man does not live by bread alone . . .'

There is one thing that holds back or slows down the efforts of men dedicated to acts of dutiful brotherly love for others.

There is something we Christians must take into consideration, something we perhaps haven't yet done: a confession we should shout out, if we don't want to be hypocrites and look like hypocrites.

Is there a materially underdeveloped Third World? This is what we must take into consideration.

Well then, there is also a Christianly, spiritually underdeveloped world.

The vast majority of us who follow Christ are really underdeveloped Christians.

Does this surprise us?

Yet it is true. The statistics of the number of baptized Christians who do not go to church make us shudder. But we do not want to speak only of those who are non-practising or who have become atheists. No: we are talking about ourselves too, and about those who, like ourselves, are called 'the faithful', 'the churchgoers', or even 'good Christians' ...

What many saints considered a true Christian is amazing, if not dismaying. Catherine of Siena, Teresa of Avila (who are both doctors of the Church), Thomas Aquinas and François de Sales, think that someone can only be spoken of as an authentic Christian, a fully actualized Christian, if he has achieved the full development of love. In fact, God's commandment, to love him with all our heart, with all our mind, is for all Christians.

After all, this conviction corresponds to the Master's often little understood words which were addressed to all: 'Be perfect as my Father is perfect.'

Commenting on this command of Jesus and explaining François de Sales' conception of the Christian life, Pope Pius XI remarked: 'No one should think that this precept is only addressed to a small number of chosen souls and that the others may keep to a lower level of virtue. It is evident that this law holds for absolutely every man without exception.'

That tiny sac that appears on the flowering apple trees when the calyxes grow and the petals have fallen, can hardly be called an apple. And when the apples have taken definite shape, but are still green and bitter, they await fresh sap and sunshine in order to be ready to fulfill the function they were created for, which is to nourish man. They still can not be called apples unless we say they are unripe apples. They are no use to man. If they fell they might be useful to animals.

We Christians are the same.

Until we are 'ripe' in our love, we cannot call ourselves Christians in the true sense of the word.

At the very start we are Christians because we are baptized. Next we are, so to speak, developing Christians. But only when the life, the law and the holiness of Christ triumph in us, can we truly call ourselves Christians.

This being the case it is not surprising that each one of us feels he is an 'underdeveloped' Christian.

What ways, what means do we have to alleviate our spiritual situation? There is no shortage. The Church offers them to us in abundance since it teaches that if baptism entitles us to the name of Christian because we are incorporated into Christ, God's grace nevertheless requires our co-operation.

We are often terribly undernourished, to such an extent that we don't feel hungry any more. And the Eucharist is there waiting for us, so that we can nourish ourselves.

We are frightfully defenceless and exposed to all sorts of spiritual diseases and often infected by one or other of them. And the sacrament of penance is there to cure and strengthen us.

We are naked and we could be clothed with Christ.

We are homeless and even here on earth we could all be in the Father's warm house, in anticipation of heaven, if we lived in that mystical but true reality of being blood relations of Christ, and of one another; and if we rediscovered ourselves as brothers, and brought the family together again with the presence of Christ among us and the circulation of material and spiritual goods among us all.

We wander like those who don't know where to go, while we have in our hands – it is enough to want it – the law of life, of every life, which is the Gospel.

We complain that today the priests are in crisis, and we are scandalized by some of their requests and we do not consider that the priest is generally the expression of the Christian society to which he belongs.

The countries of the Third World are genuinely economically underdeveloped.

We Christians are stupidly underdeveloped because the possibilities of development are all around us, and yet we are in imminent danger of starvation, like King Midas surrounded by his gold.

The problems of the Third World are very serious.

What is needed is a massive transfer of goods, a restructuring, a major overhaul.

And we do not know how to do all this.

We are not able to work out comprehensive plans for the whole world, not even in order to help it, because this would require a universal love.

For this we must have the collaboration of the one who created this world, who knows its destinies, and who penetrates the most hidden thoughts of men, their aspirations and the spiritual and material capacities of peoples. He who knows this humanity by direct experience also, he who sums up mankind because he is not just a man but Man : he alone can set alight in us a spirit and a universal vision of Love.

Pope John XXIII, for instance, told us we should measure the surplus we give to others by the extent of their need.

But who will measure the need of all our brothers except some one who has in himself the measure of mankind? Only Christ has this measure.

And, in general, he wants to act in the world through Christians. And he can do this with those in whom, filled with love, he fully lives and acts.

Then the plans they make will be illuminated by his wisdom and will be carried out despite all the difficulties.

I think that if we really want to solve the problems of the Third World, we have an urgent need to solve our own more serious problem, our being only faintly Christian.

Going back to the earlier example – as the apple fulfills its function only when it is ripe, the Christian is truly, decisively, adequately useful to mankind when he is 'perfect like the Father', because when he is perfect like the

Father he is another Christ and, therefore, another 'Son of Man'.

This is wonderful because it means that only a true Christian can become a perfect man.

But that is not enough. We have to draw out all the consequences. Authenticity, the characteristic of our times requires it: the perfect Christian is also a saint.

So we must conclude that: in God's eyes 'man', 'Christian', 'saint' are synonymous.

'Holiness! That's only a word,' say many, very many people.

No. Christ has not asked the impossible of us.

And we must get rid of a certain notion of holiness that is prevalent among people. Phenomena, such as miracles, ecstacies and visions do not constitute holiness.

Holiness consists of perfect love.

And today, when the masses are awakening – and this is a sign of the times – today also, when people must have brotherly relations with one another and every detail has to be seen from a world viewpoint, what is needed is a mass holiness, a communal holiness, a popular holiness.

68

LIGHT A LIVING CELL

IF YOU LOOK around you in some cities you pass through, you are left dismayed and it seems to you that the realization of a Christian society is far off. The world with its vanity seems to dominate . . .

And you would call the testament of Jesus a utopia if you did not think of him. He saw a world like this too, and at the climax of his life he appeared to be overcome by it, defeated by evil.

He, too, looked at all that crowd which he loved as himself. He, God, who had created it. And he would have liked to build the bonds which were going to bring them together as sons of the Father, and unite brother with brother.

He came to bring the family together again: to make all one.

Instead, despite his words of fire and truth – that burned away the happiness of vanity, uncovering the eternal that is in man – the people, many people, even though they understood, did not want to know and remained with lifeless eyes because their soul was dark.

This was because he had made them free. Having come from heaven to earth, he could have saved them all with just a glance. But he had to leave to them, who were made in the image of God, the joy of freely winning salvation.

He looked on the world just as we see it, but did not doubt.

At night he prayed heaven above and heaven within himself: the Trinity that is true Being, the real All, while outside the nothingness that passes away moved through the streets.

We, too, must do as he did and not be parted from the Eternal, from the Uncreated that is the root of the created, and we must believe in the final victory of light over darkness.

We must pass through the world and not wish to look at it. We must look at the heaven that is also in us and attach ourselves to what has being and value. We must make ourselves completely one with the Trinity who dwells in our soul, enlightening it with eternal light.

Then you will notice, with eyes which are no

longer lifeless, that you look at the world and at things, but that it is no longer you looking at it: it is Christ who looks, and in you he sees again the blind needing sight, the dumb to be made to speak, the crippled to be made to walk, people who are blind to the vision of God inside and outside them, people who are immobile and crippled because they are unaware of the divine will which, from the bottom of their hearts spurs them on to the eternal movement that is eternal love.

You see and discover your own light in them: your true self, which is Christ, the true reality of you in them, and having found him, you unite with him in your brother. So you light a cell of the Body of Christ, a living cell, a hearth of God where there is fire to communicate to others and with it light. It is God who makes two one, and who places himself as a third, as the relation between them: Jesus among them.

In this way love circulates and spontaneously carries with it, like a river in flood, everything else the two own, both their spiritual and their material goods. This is the practical and out-ward witness of true, unifying love.

But we need to have the courage not to bother

too much about other means if we want to revive a little bit of Christianity.

We must make God live in us and pour him out over others like a stream of life, reviving the lifeless.

And keep him alive among us by loving one another.

Then everything around is revolutionized: politics and art, school and work, private life and entertainment. Everything.

Jesus is the perfect man who contains all men and recapitulates every truth.

Whoever has found this man has found the answer to every human and divine problem.

A MOTHER DOES not stop loving her son if he is bad, she does not stop waiting for him if he is far away, her one desire is to meet him again, to forgive him, to embrace him again because the love of a mother embraces everything with mercy.

The love of a mother is something that is always above whatever sad condition or painful situation her child may find himself in.

It is a love that never gives away in the face of any moral, ideological or other kind of storm that can overcome her child.

Her love is a love that desires to cover and to hide everything, because it stands above everything.

If a mother sees her own child in danger she has no hesitation about risking everything. She is ready to throw herself on the tracks in front of a train if her child is in danger of being run over by it, or to throw herself into the sea if her child is in danger of drowning, because the love of a mother is by nature stronger than death.

It was reported recently that a mother flung herself from her balcony in an attempt to save her baby that had slipped from her arms: a useless act of despair, but it shows how great a mother's love is.

If this is true of ordinary mothers, we can imagine how true it is of Mary, the human-divine mother of the baby that was God, and the spiritual mother of us all!

Mary is the mother *par excellence*, the model of motherhood and, therefore, of human love.

But since God is *Love*, she is an 'explanation' of God, an open book that explains God.

The love in God was so great that he died the most atrocious death for us, in order to save us: just as the motive for a mother's love is the good of her child.

Mary, because she is the divine Mother, is the creature who copies God most and shows him most to us.

We must revive our faith in Mary's love for us, we ought to believe that she loves us like this. We must imitate her because she is the model for every Christian and the quickest way that leads to God.

THE PEARL

JESUS WHO ANNIHILATES himself on the
cross, in that utter poverty, in that absolute
void, is truly the most precious pearl.

Seeking to live him again in ourselves, we are
nothing but love, because we are nothing of
ourselves; in order to be his will for us, we do
not exist for ourselves so as to be charity towards others, who in that emptiness can pour
out the fullness of their heart.

In this way, freed from their distresses, from
their pressing worries, they also come to possess
in their turn a soul which is free and open, in
which we can place the seed of the love of God
which will then fall on good ground.

This is the way the Kingdom of Heaven
spreads, the kingdom that must spread, the
kingdom whose coming we pray for every morning.

A PARADOXICAL FUNCTION

IN THE ACTS, in the duties of our day, we must
know how to appreciate, moment by moment,
the unpleasantness they entail, we have to high-
light and value the wearisome aspect, the
amount of fatigue, of discomfort, of effort, of
toil, so that we can welcome all this as a precious possession to be given to God.

Everything that tastes of suffering is, in fact,
extremely important.

The world does not want to hear suffering
mentioned, partly because since it is no longer
Christian it does not understand it, and partly
because it is natural that suffering does not
please. So the world avoids it and wants to forget it.

Yet suffering has a paradoxical function: it is
the channel of happiness, if by happiness we
mean the true and enduring kind, not the temp-
orary fleeting sort. This happiness sates the
human heart, because it is the very same happi-

ness that God enjoys and Man can share in it already in this life through his transcendent destiny.

Just as Jesus, precisely through suffering, gave joy to men on earth and unending joy in the next life, so man, through the various worries accepted and offered every day with a supernatural spirit, can obtain happiness for himself and for others.

IN THIS WAY WE ARE HUMBLE

HUMILITY IS A virtue that attracts and fascin-
ates.

It tells us what we are and what God is.

We, of ourselves, are nothing.

We will live humility well if we can live this
nothing of ourselves and the everything of God.

We can do this only if we live his will in the
present: in this way we are humble.

The aspiration of every man is to be God.

John of the Cross says: 'What God desires is to
make us gods by participation, being himself
God by nature . . .'

God by participation: Being by participation.

I would like to be Being, so that Being may
speak of itself to the world every moment.

This will happen if I now manage not to be
myself, my will, my thought.

This is what Mary must have been like.

LOVE MAKES US SEE

FAITH IS THREATENED in our times. This protest is not a joke.

It happened to me, too, that while reading one of these 'modern' religious books, doubt about faith entered my mind. I realized the disaster this would have caused if I had stopped to consider the doubt: all that inner life which with God's grace I had been building up over these years would have crumbled. And I remembered that Jesus calls 'blessed' those who believe without seeing.

So, just as I had been taught from my infancy, I chased that doubt away, and the inner life, with the peace only God is able to give, began to flow normally again.

Today more than ever, since many principles of faith are disputed, we must anchor ourselves to the rock of infallibility; to the Pope, to what he says, and to the bishops, united with him. Besides, even St Paul in his exhausting work of evangelizing the pagan world, must have known the struggle to keep the integrity of the faith. It is notable that at the end of his life he mentions among his just merits: 'I have kept the faith.'

We Christians will succeed in imitating him if we are faithful to our first vocation: that of loving. No bulwark for the defence of the faith seems to me better than love. Because love 'make us see', love 'manifests', with the result that faith is strengthened.

After all, we too, should our faith waver, would have to say with Peter: 'To whom shall we go? You alone have the words of eternal life.'

IT IS IMPORTANT to live the Christian ideal in depth because, if we look around, we see that everything calls for it: the need for freedom, for self-affirmation, for group life, for participation, for dialogue, for authenticity. All this and even more is in the Christian ideal.

The truth, Christ, sets us truly *free* from everything and from ourselves.

Then the deepest unity between us distinguishes us as new men with the maximum affirmation of the divine and human personality of each of us.

If we have Christ among us we can be the most exemplary *group* because we are cells of his Body, the Church.

We can live the fullest *participation* because unity does not exist without a complete love for all, with a giving of all ourselves.

We are able to initiate a constructive *dialogue*, modelled a little on the life of the Holy

81

Trinity, where the divine Persons are eternally one and in loving dialogue.

We are able to have *authenticity* because, purified by truth of the dross of the old man, it is no longer we who live but Christ in us, who is our true self.

THE LOVE THAT MAKES US
BROTHERS

IN THE POPE'S message for the World Day of Peace, to 'all men living in 1972', there is a passage near the end addressed to the brothers and children of our Catholic Church, and in it the Pope invites us to 'bring to men a message of hope by means of a *lived brotherhood* and an honest and persevering effort for greater real justice.'

I want to consider for a moment this request the Pope makes to his children to offer the world a lived brotherhood, in order to see how we can put it into practice and give mankind a message of hope.

First of all, we can ask ourselves: is there among us Catholics a basis for creating a more heartfelt brotherhood? And further: is today's world open to this?

If we look at the Church and mankind, we'll see how both are subject to two contrasting tensions.

The Church today, too – as in every age, since it has the same destiny as its Founder – walks along a way of the cross. A frenzy of new ideas seems to menace the roots of faith and morality, raising doubts about everyone and everything. An overall protest estranges some of the Church's best sons, impoverishing it by the loss of even those chosen and sent in its name to announce the Gospel. The hierarchy itself is at times put on trial by those who, because they want to humanize everything, disregard the value of the ecclesiastical magisterium.

Mankind, in which the Church lives and whose every tremor strongly affects it, is torn by division and by the unleashing of the instincts against every form of order and every structure that might bind everyone together. Then there are the social imbalances, the continual outbreaks of war that keep men with bated breath in terror of a world conflict and all those moral evils of today that we know. In short: disorientation in every field.

However, we can see parallel to this tragic but true picture, a vague but felt desire for *brotherhood*, for unity that surmounts existing barriers and aims at the world taken as a whole.

Unity that is not just an aspiration but which, in the political field for example, is already a realization in different forms, all inspired legitimately or not, by the testament of Jesus, and at the same time there is an increase in the number of nations which hope to resolve the gravest tensions in a peaceful way. In the social field, the air is vibrating with a sense of solidarity, which adults and especially young people, are feeling. And along with so much bad news which is published, there is the recent surprising phenomenon of great numbers of young people rebelling in the name of Christ against the slavery of sex and drugs.

In the Church, the Pentecost of the Council continues to raise its authoritative voice above the world's whisper and gives it hope again : a voice that calls on the divine to shine out and make this earth come alive, and on faith freed of incidentals to confirm itself again more beautifully and more truly : a voice which urges the moral order to re-establish itself to save man from his own ruin, which exhorts social structures to be christianized, priests to be light in the world, bishops to co-operate with the Pope so that unity in diversity may shine forth

85

all the more. And there is the clear, strong and sure voice of the Pope who, in order to instruct and 'to confirm his brothers', constantly announces the truth and puts forward again the Council's teaching, clarifying it for the people of God.

Yet another attractive and present-day characteristic of the Church stands out: varied charisms of the Holy Spirit are echoing the desires of the Holy Spirit in the Second Vatican Council, calling on Christians to be Church in the deepest meaning of the word, that is communion, lived brotherhood. From this comes a revival of movements of different origins animated by a marked sense of brotherhood, existing in a world that is calling out for this, but often in the name of those who do not know how to really give this brotherhood. These groups sometimes do not themselves know how to measure what power they possess precisely because they are Christians.

To form a brotherhood you need love. And by now this is known to everyone in the world to a greater or lesser degree. The Muslims too, who do not believe in the Trinitarian God but only in the One God are, in different areas, responsive to a brotherhood based on love.

But the love that a Christian brings – and here is the utterly deep mystery and hidden power that once made fruitful can work miracles – is different from any other love existing in the world, however noble and beautiful it may be. It is a love of divine origin, God's very own love shared with Man, who being grafted in him, becomes a son of God.

This is the boundary and cause of an incomparable reality: human brotherhood on a higher level, *supernatural brotherhood*.

It is in *this* brotherhood that an event occurs which reminds us of Christmas: Christ is born among men as Emmanuel, God with us. In this brotherhood Christians are united in the name of Christ who said: 'Where two or three have met together in my name, I am there among them' (Mt. 18, 20). It is a kind of brotherhood that can – even where the Church finds itself obstructed in its ministry – make Christ present among men. Spiritually present, that is, but present. It is this brotherhood that can bring Christ among the people, into homes, into schools, into hospitals, into factories, into every community or meeting.

The Council and the Pope stress this several times: the community united like a family in the name of the Lord enjoys his presence. It is a question of the brotherhood that makes us Church, as Odo Casel points out: 'It is not that the single Church fragments into a plurality of different communities, nor that the multiplicity of different communions united together forms the single Church. The Church is only *one*, wherever it appears, it is all entire and undivided, even where only two or three are gathered in the name of Christ.'

Now maybe we Christians do not always take account of this extraordinary possibility. By our acknowledging it this Christmas, God will be able to give us the grace to welcome and to make more fruitful such a gift.

In this brotherhood, everywhere and with everyone, we need not anxiously think how we can sort out human problems on our own. If we so wish (and it is enough to be united in his name, that is in him and in the way he wishes), Christ is among us and with us, he, the Almighty! This gives us hope. Yes, it gives us great hope.

We must revive a little in our Christian families, in our groups, in our movements, whatever their aim provided they are Christian, and in the activities to which we dedicate our efforts, that unity, that brotherhood that makes Christ present among us and makes us Church, openly declaring to one another this desire of ours, without any fear of false modesty.

If Christmas reminds us to what extent God has loved us, and that is, to the point of making himself one of us, it is easy to understand how the logic of his love makes him always want to be a partner in our doings and desirous to live in a certain way among us, sharing our happiness, our griefs, responsibilities and weariness, above all giving us a hand as our brother. For him, it is not enough to represent himself to us every time we solemnly join together for the Eucharistic celebration, or to be particularly present in other ways such as in the hierarchy or in his word ... he wishes to be with us *always*. And all he needs are two or three Christians ... and they don't have to be saints already! All that is needed are two or more men of good will who believe in him and especially in his love.

If we do this, there will be an upsurge of

living cells in the Church which, in time, will be able to animate the society that surrounds them until they penetrate the whole mass. This mass, then, informed by the spirit of Christ, will be better able to fulfil God's plan for the world, and give a decisive thrust to the peaceful, irresistible social revolution, with consequences we'd never dared hoped for.

If the historic Christ healed and satisfied the hunger of souls and bodies, Christ mystically present among his own knows how to do just as much now. If the historic Christ asked his Father, before dying, for oneness among his disciples, Christ mystically present among Christians knows how to bring this about.

To help us respond to all that God is asking of us through the Pope, much seems to have been prepared for us by the Holy Spirit. We need to give new impetus to our Christian life which is always too individualistic, often mediocre, but above all, lacking in authenticity.

GOLDEN THOUGHTS

IT IS NOT to think of black but of golden thoughts that we think of death. Even among an abundance of graces, sometimes we are seized by the sense of the loneliness of exile on earth, and we find ourselves wanting to say again with Paul: 'I should like to depart and be with Christ, which is a far better thing,' or 'We would rather leave our home in the body and go to live with the Lord.'

The more we appreciate and go into the depths of suffering, the more we also understand that death is the ultimate offering of ourselves as 'royal priests' here on earth and, therefore, the culmination of our lives. For whoever loves and knows what it means to love, it is the desired moment.

I would like to explain what I mean.

It is really 'desired' in the sense that gold is desired and smoke is not. In short, a moment kissed by God, as Jesus crucified is kissed.

Our Christian brothers who have died and have lived the moment of death know what it is. Oh! how often we would like some one to have come and told us something about this 'passing' . . .

But perhaps – no, certainly, because this, too, is love – it is better that each one of us should go through this unique experience in life : it has more value and . . . for the little suffering, for the little faith we have in God's love for us in those moments, then for all eternity we will be with him.

THE ESSENTIAL IS MISSING

WE ARE IN LENT.

Why is it so difficult to talk about penance in our modern times?

Good people, in certain areas, especially country people, and above all, women, still accept the parish priest's invitation to penance. And do it.

We hear of pilgrimages entailing bodily sufferings which throngs of Christians make to Fatima and to Lourdes, and they are not usually fanatical people.

The fact is that, despite the survival of these events, for Christians today in general the word *penance* has rather fallen into disuse.

And perhaps this is right. Perhaps it is fortunate because it warns us that to add a penance to the Christian life as it is being lived (or rather as it is not being lived), is like cultivating a flower in a pot destined for the balcony of a house that is not yet built.

We can feel that the greater part, the essential, is missing, and that, therefore, the lesser part, the accessory, has no meaning.

Because the Christian life is to do God's will and the Christian often does his own or does God's, but unwillingly ...

Because to be Christians means to love even our enemies. But who thinks of that? It is already a lot if we avoid revenge ...

Because to be Christians means to love each other, to be one heart and one soul with the other Christians, but that is too difficult ... Each person thinks of himself and then he has enough to do.

Because to be Christians means to obey the Church, and to obey those who represent it and their directives. But today it is old fashioned to obey, and the Church is not too convincing ...

Because ... because ... because ...

How much is missing that should be normal in our Christian life *before* adding on something particular like a penance.

And yet, Pope John, who certainly was not out of touch with his age, but attracted the world with his goodness, says age-old things which, however, reacquire all their vitality, because expressed by *those* lips, suggested by *that* heart, and firstly lived by *that* truly fully Christian soul and then made public. And because they are truths expressed by him, they become fashionable again.

He states that: 'In addition to the penances we necessarily have to meet with in the inevitable sufferings of this mortal life, Christians should be so generous as to offer to God voluntary mortification as well, following the example of our divine Redeemer ... In this the saints of the Church are also an example and an encouragement; the mortifications they inflicted on their often most innocent bodies fill us with wonder and almost perplexity. Faced with these champions of Christian holiness, how can we not refuse to the Lord some deprivation or voluntary pain even on behalf of the faithful, who perhaps have so many faults to atone for?'

WE GO TO God through our brother. 'He who does not love his brother whom he has seen cannot love God whom he has never seen.'

Today, in times like ours, the Christian must keep this above all in mind.

Sometimes the materialism which surrounds us and the temptations it arouses, the gossip and discussions which attract those who are itching to hear, the mania for being informed, for knowing everything, for reading everything and the resulting attachment to something considered quite legitimate, all distract our attention from what our *brother* awaits from us.

Instead, it is all here. 'Before all else have mutual and continual love' with others.

Scripture says: 'We have passed out of death and in *to life* . . . because we love our brothers,' not for other reasons.

We are called to live and to bring *life*, even if this brotherly love costs us a continual effort. But this is nothing more than the cross which characterizes the Christian.

OUR HEART MUST BE OPEN TO BOTH

WHEN IN LIFE the shadow of suffering arrives, we return to *reality*, which is natural and supernatural life. In fact, it is then that we return more easily to God, should we have wandered away from him a little.

When suffering is missing, we often delude ourselves with what is *transitory*.

However, suffering should not drown the soul in bitterness which prevents us seeing all the gifts offered to us by God, including his many gifts to us each day, since it is characteristic of the Christian to have the hundredfold in this life even in the midst of persecutions.

God wants us to thank him for both the hundredfold and for the suffering, and so our heart must be open to both.

For whoever has understood that the cross is essential to the Christian life and, therefore, loves it, suffering loses its weight and becomes light and easy, something he is able for, and it assumes its rightful proportions. In fact, in this case the cross is carried by two people: God and ourselves.

Only by living like this can we see and taste the beauty and the consolation that runs parallel to the daily pain. Suffering, then, has a very important function: it helps to keep us in the *supernatural* life.

JOYS AND SORROWS,
hopes,
dreams come true.
Maturity of life and of thought.
Solidity.
Sense of duty.
And the call of love from above,
answered by
the coherence of our life.
Weariness.
Flames and conquests.
Storms.
Trust in God:
God alone.
Up.
Down.
Torrential downpours,
deep roots.
Fruits, fruits, fruits . . .
Overclouding of the soul:

'My God, my God . . .'
Then, sweet music from heaven,
in the distance.
Then nearer.
Drums roll:
Victory!

Life is long,
Varied the road,
the goal is near.
All,
everything,
every single thing,
always,
has,
has had,
one destiny only:
union with You.

WHOEVER LOVES, REIGNS

WHOEVER LOVES, REIGNS. This is so true.

It is true for you too, and for anyone who is poor or sick and meets people who are rich and full of health.

Because whoever loves, gives, always gives.

And it is this giving of his that he is king and has in himself the fullness that has no end.

Perhaps this why God has commanded us to love: to give us the joy of feeling that we are children not of limited and ineffective men, but of God, of the King of kings.

THEY KNOW GOD

'HE WHO DOES not love has not known God because God is love.' The Church's athletes are those who *love* God, because they know him and knowing him they defend him, defending faith in him.

UNINTERRUPTED LIFE

WHEN YOU SUDDENLY find yourself faced with disaster, you hear the echo of the words of scripture: 'Everything is vanity of vanities.'

Yes, everything passes.

Creatures pass, health passes, beauty passes, things pass . . . God remains.

It is the time to choose him again as the only ideal of your life and, consistent with your choice, to live in the way he commands.

Love.

By loving you will understand many things and you will then see the golden thread of your life which seemed to have been interrupted by that abrupt event, continue to shine as brightly and more brightly than before.

Because life can undergo interruptions, but God-Life always lives and so do those who have grafted and regrafted their own lives on to the God-Life.

104

'LOVE YOUR NEIGHBOUR as yourself.' This is a continual tension because our nature loves itself.

Often we hear news of disasters, earthquakes, hurricanes, which claim victims and leave people injured and homeless.

But it is one thing to be one of them, and another thing to be one of us.

Even if we are able to offer some aid to help the others, we are not them.

Tomorrow it could be the other way round. I, on my deathbed (if I am given a bed!), and the others out in the sun enjoying life as best they can.

'Love your neighbour as yourself': all that Christ has commanded us goes beyond our nature as it is now.

But also the *gift* that he has made us, the one mentioned to the Samaritan woman, is not human in nature.

So it is possible to share in our brother's pain, joy or worries because we have in us charity which is of a divine nature.

With *this* love, that is with Christian love, our brother can be really comforted, and tomorrow I can be comforted by him. And in such a way as this, it is possible to *live*, because otherwise human life would be rather hard and difficult, and could appear at times to be impossible.

EVERY MOMENT HAS ITS CROSS

WE LEARN BY living in the present moment, that if we live it well, it is always possible to carry out the words of Christ: 'Take up your cross.' Almost every moment has its cross: tiny, small or great, spiritual or physical sufferings accompany our life in the present. We have to 'take up' these crosses, not try to forget them by escaping into an uncommitted life.

And also, should everything be health and joy, it is advisable, while being grateful to God, to live detached from this and not fall back avidly on the gift rather than on the Giver, and then remain sad with emptiness in our soul.

COMMITTED TO MANKIND

SOMETIMES PEOPLE HAVE been given the impression – as we Christans are often accused of doing – that by living our faith consistently that is, in view of the life to come and in expectation of death which is the doorway to it we lead an existence which is a bit detached from the earth, and uncommitted to the interests of this world, which often represent the good of mankind.

The reality is that if we always live in the deep awareness of knowing 'neither the day nor the hour', we concentrate more easily on the 'today' which we have been given, on today's troubles, on the present moment which providence gives us to live. And in the present we welcome and we live joys and sorrows, efforts and results, with all our being.

This is how the life of this earth is *truly* lived. While, on the contrary, without the prospect that sooner or later we have to go away from here, we often lead a superficial existence based on illusions, on dreams, on something we are always aiming at, but which perhaps will never be achieved.

Living the present in this way does not lead us to forget the earthly future or to clip the wings of our planning for our own good and that of others: for our children, for our family, for the community in which we live, for mankind.

Living the present this way does not make us forget the past with its heritage of thoughts, of heroic deeds, of conquests.

Christians, in fact, if they really are Christians, cannot help having in their hearts love towards all men. This is their nature, their prerogative: raised to being sons of God, they possess love *par excellence,* the same love Christ has for the Father: charity.

Through charity Christians feel inserted in the whole of mankind like small stones in a marvellous mosiac, which is complete in some parts but not in others.

They love the mankind of the past in the same way as the mankind of tomorrow.

They approach what has been handed down

by mankind with the respect of one who knows he is drawing near to someone or something belonging to him, with the humility of someone who is convinced he has to learn, conscious that he must transmit it, enriched by his own personal commitment, to the future generations.

If then, in the present moment of their life Christians realize that God wants them to think of tomorrow, they do so with complete commitment, not for themselves but for love of those who will come after them – whether they are known to them or not.

This feeling of being one with mankind, past, present and future, this love for others as oneself, is for the Christian the powerful force that makes him fit and strong for building today, and for planning a better life for the future.

In short, it is precisely the prospect of the other life and the observance of the rules for getting there, concentrated in the commandment of love towards all, that makes not only perfect Christians but authentic men, the way that the modern age and today's society wants them to be, but above all the way God wants them to be in this century.

110

SUFFERING MAKES US SEE

THE CROSS, SUFFERING, especially continued suffering, is one of the greatest gifts God can give us. Immersed in it, we are as if transferred into the darkness of the stratosphere where distant things can be seen more clearly.

When the cross is absent, it is easy to fool ourselves into thinking that fireflies are stars, and we make concessions to our own ego, to our own conceit, believing everything to be in the service of God, compatible with and even useful for his glory. The result is that we offer him a life that is a mixture of incense and smoke.

On the other hand, when suffering visits us and we do not draw away from it, we understand the words of the saints which invite us to hiddenness, to nothingness, to authenticity in the face of men and in the face of God. This awareness can be so strong that sincere acts of gratitude to him who permits suffering arise from the depths of your soul.

The cross makes you sure of being on the right way, guarantees you that everything is going well because the diameter of the roots of the tree of your life is widening out: a sure sign that the foliage, too, is opening out in a new beauty.

You realize that the beatitudes Christ announced are not words of mere encouragement, or only promises, but reality. And that for he who weeps, it is not impossible, in fact, that in that very weeping he should feel himself 'blessed'. A beatitude different from that to come, but a real beatitude.

IT IS VERY wise to spend the time we have by living perfectly the will of God in the present moment.

Sometimes, however, we are assailed by such worrying thoughts, whether they regard the past, the future or the present, concerning places or circumstances or people we cannot directly dedicate ourselves to, that it takes the greatest effort to steer the ship of our life, keeping to the course God wishes of us in *that* present moment.

Then, to live perfectly, we need a will, a decision, but above all, a *confidence* in God that can reach an heroic degree.

'I can do nothing in this case for that dear person who is sick or in danger, for that complicated situation . . .'

'Well then, I will do what God wants of me in this moment: study well, sweep well, pray well, take care of my children well . . .'

'And God will see to the untangling of this

113

knot, comforting the one who is suffering, sorting out that unexpected event.'

It is a job done by two people in perfect communion, that demands from us great faith in God's love for his children and that makes it possible, through our action, for God himself to have trust in us.

This reciprocal confidence works miracles.

We will see that what we could not do, an Other has truly done, and has done far better than us.

The heroic act of confidence will be rewarded, our life limited to one field only, will acquire a new dimension, we will feel in contact with the infinite, for which we yearn, and faith taking on a new vigour will strengthen the love, the charity in us.

We will no longer remember what loneliness means. The reality that we are truly children of a God-Father who can do everything, will become clearer to us because we also have experienced it.

I AM THE WATER OF THIS SPRING

WE OFTEN MAKE resolutions, and we do not always manage to keep them.

But in some rare instances we notice that it is not we who make them. It is an Other who calls in us, gently but decisively. Then it seems we cannot help keeping them.

We have to thank God for these divine moments in which he calls us to the other life that lives within us, where every note is in harmony, every darkness is lit up, every fold is straightened, every void is filled with him. This can happen at any moment of the day.

We feel that there are two of us: he in me and I in him. Yet we are one: I am the water of this spring, the flower of this divine seed, the witness of his reality that fills my being.

This really is life.

God alone, in fact, can shape himself in us. We can only ruin him.

JESUS, ON EASTER morning, you appear to Magdalene and call her by name. You have forgotten everything about her: her sins, her past.

You call her.

Then the same applies to each of us too.

If we have decided to love you, you do not remember a thing. You call us by name.

How can we be worried about our failures, then, about our past, about our sins?

Are you not now the same Jesus as then?

A NEED OF THE HEART

WHEN SOMEONE YOU love, a relative or a friend, comes to visit you, you are often worried about what present to give them. You look around, flick through books, open drawers and see if you have ... I don't know; some little thing, a box of sweets; you buy a pot of flowers, or something to wear that would suit them, you choose a picture, a knick-knack, something ...

That's what happens. And it is no bother: it is a need of the heart.

One phrase in the Gospel that strongly impresses us when we come across it is this: 'Whatever you ask for in prayer, believe that you have received it and it will be yours.'

Jesus repeated so often in various ways that 'ask', 'knock', 'ask in my name', and always, in every one of these words, we perceive his love for us.

But the phrase in which he adds 'Believe you

have already received it' is even stronger ...

He wants us to believe we have already obtained the grace even before we have asked for it.

It is a paradox. It unveils all the love with which Christ loves us and loves me.

But the certainty of his measureless love becomes rock-like when in serious or almost desperate moments, you have tried to ask with 'that' faith and have really received.

And not just once.

Christ, his human-divine heart, all powerful, perhaps desires nothing more than to make his brothers share in the inexhaustible treasures he has at his disposal.

A NOTE OF SOLEMNITY

IF SOMEONE BEGINS or begins again to live the present moment well in their life, you will notice in time that, even if they have not set out to do so, their actions have taken on a note of solemnity. Through this you can see that that brother's life rests on a single supernatural support: *love for God.*

At the same time, however, this note of continuity characterizes deeply each of his activities to such an extent that it makes his existence very distinctive, and it follows that his spiritual character becomes focused with growing precision.

You can say of him, for example, that he is: *immersed* in God in prayer; *free* and *cheerful* in company; *exact* in his duty; *demanding* with himself; *fraternal* with everyone; *intransigent* in the disciplining of those who depend on him; *merciful* to those who fall; that he has a rock-like *conviction* of his own nothingness and of

God's all powerfulness; is often *dissatisfied* with his own behaviour, and is always *ready*, however, to hope and to begin again.

It is precisely this eternal beginning again required by human life weakened by original sin, that helps the soul to clothe itself in that note of continuity while carrying out a variety of actions. This is the perfume of the soul, at first a little, then more and more.

Because someone who lives no longer in himself, in his own will, but is transferred into the will of the Other, is holy.

FOR THE CHRISTIAN, it is not *how much* he does, but *how* he does it, that counts.

Not even the historical Jesus changed the world. At times, in fact, he seemed to fail. What is important is to fulfill the plan God has for us – no more, but certainly no less.

Let us work at our job, adoring his will which binds us not only to the present moment in time, but also to a single detail of the task we must achieve in the world

Certainly, if we are disunited, like a lot of separate pieces, we will have the impression that we are achieving precious little. But if we are united, what one does is seen in connection with all that the others are doing. And then every action will take on a dimension and a quality which is not just universal – the universe is small compared with heaven – but is heavenly.

Let us love then that smile we give, that job we do, that car we drive, that meal we prepare, that activity we organize, that tear we shed for Christ in our brother who is suffering, that instrument we play, that article or letter we write, that happy event we share joyfully, that suit we clean ...

Everything, everything can become a means to show our love to God and to our brothers. Everything has been entrusted into our hands and into our hearts, like the crucifix given to missionaries, for the evangelization we have to carry out in the world.

A UNIQUE EXPERIENCE

I WENT TO Subiaco to go to confession. I was
not able to tour the abbey. There wasn't time.

I had hardly entered when I was deeply
touched by the charity of the doorkeeper: a
little brother, old and lame, who wanted to accompany me to the church.

In confession, however, I had a unique experience: I was touched from the very first
words of that holy monk.

It is difficult to explain what happened, and
yet it can be said quickly: I met God.

From the soul of that priest a spring seemed
to flow that had its origins sixteen centuries ago
in Benedict and the pierced side of Christ the
Saviour.

I wanted to stay in that church for ever in
the grasp of a deep emotion.

I envied that austere life that has openly and
decisively broken with the world.

Now I understand why the abbeys survive

with the centuries and are eternally modern: men live here who already dwell in heaven, and they communicate that atmosphere to you sweetly, so that it completely penetrates you.

I saw our Christian life in contrast as being very difficult: always in contact with a world devoid of God, always with occasions for compromise, because we are frightened, sometimes, of the hatred that must come.

Only a strongly committed inner life, fully involved in the will of God in the present moment, can make us also hope to be bearers of God and not of words.

One monk is worth more than a community of a thousand good persons not in perfect unity, not fully afire with love for God and for men.

Saint Benedict can be satisfied.

Now that I have found living gold in the Benedictines of Subiaco, one day, if God wills, I will go to visit the monastery and its walls which are the witnesses of such holiness.

NOSTALGIA FOR THE DIVINE

I AM WALKING along a street in a big city. It is almost impossible to move forward: the devil is ruler here, and he has soiled everything. Half-naked women, drugged youths, sickening immorality: world, world, world, world.

In the space of only five or six years, the whole appearance of these streets seems to have changed.

Even the beautiful mountains have been ruined: all 'mod. cons.' are provided at the six thousand feet level, and along with these come more and more people. Everyone tries to outdo the others by wearing outlandish clothes, and it seems that no one has any taste at all. Extravagance is used to attract attention.

A tiny Alpine chapel, of which I caught a glimpse from the ski-lift, bears witness to the reality which this generation ignores, and which only a few old folk seem to acknowledge.

When I reach the top, I withdraw to a corner

of the bar in the immense hotel which, like a great concrete barracks, entirely covers the summit. In this way I will be able to have a little nook where I can collect my thoughts and clean off the dust that begrimes the soul. But the barman informs me that loitering is not allowed.

I am assailed by a great sadness and an immense nostalgia for the divine. The world seems like a monster with claws, not letting me breathe.

I know Christ has left me in the world ... but: 'Enough, enough – I almost cried out – I can't take any more.'

I confide in a friend who is with me. I understand that the self-denial which Christ asks of his followers is a comforting deliverance; that the counsels of the Gospels, which at least spiritually all Christians are called to follow, are the angel's wings by which we can walk through these filthy streets. Nowadays, too, two thousand years later, we often have to turn our gaze away from what we come across, to have only a little money so as not to be tempted to spend, and to bring our own will into line with God's.

And often I am assailed by nostalgia for places where everything has been ordered by inspiration from God in the rules of the saints: the monasteries, where we can enter already here on earth the joy of heaven.

But this is not possible. Like me, there are millions of people called by Christ to be his and to stay in the world without becoming contaminated by it.

Then it is not enough to detest evil. We must radiate goodness, we must *love*.

The best medicine for this sick and wretched society is not only to try to pull down its strongholds which are often reduced to faded illusions. Today, just as it did twenty centuries ago, Christianity must spread light and the darkness will retreat, it must spread love, charity, goodness and human perversion will go away.

Christ must grow in us and among us and we must never be afraid, even though we are a little scattered flock.

SANCTIFYING OURSELVES AS CHURCH

AS CAN EASILY be observed, the deep desire, the urgency, I would call it, to serve the Church, is growing among Christians, but not so much and not only in an external and material manner, as in various ways more in tune with their faith and more essential.

You notice that, especially among lay people, the way of sanctifying oneself as it has been conceived up to now, makes little impression and is sometimes even considered outmoded. The style of holiness of today's Christian goes beyond that of an individually sought perfection, and is often expressed like this: we wish to become holy together, we want a collective holiness.

So here and there groups of committed Christians are being formed, who united go towards God.

Well, it seems to us that it is God who wills this, provided it all has a full character, the dimension of the Church, and loving union with the hierarchy.

The face of the Church, here transparent with light, there darkened by shadows, should be reflected in each Christian, in every group of Christians: which means we must feel as our own not only all the joys of the Church, its hopes, its ever new flowerings, its conquests, but especially we must feel as our own all its sufferings: the traumatic one of the separation between the Churches, the wounds of painful situations, of negative disputes, of the threatened destruction of centuries-old treasures; the anguish of those who are far from the Church, the atheists, who deny or do not accept the message God announces to the world for its salvation.

In all these griefs, particularly in the spiritual ones, the suffering Church appears as the crucified one of our days crying: 'My God, my God, why have you forsaken me?'

A while ago I was at La Verna. I meditated there on the exceptional gift of the stigmata that God gave Francis as a mark of his imitation of Christ, of his being Christian.

I thought, all true Christians ought to be stigmatized, not indeed in the extraordinary and external sense, but spiritually.

And I seemed to understand that the stigmata of the Christians of our days are exactly the mysterious but real wounds of the Church today.

If the charity of Christ is not developed enough in us to make us experience the suffering of these wounds, we are not as God wants us to be today.

At this time, a holiness that is too individual, or which is even communal but closed, is not enough.

We need to experience in ourselves the feelings of sorrow and also of joy that Christ in his Bride experiences today.

We need to sanctify ourselves as Church.

ON TIPTOE

IF WE ARE happy to announce the Kingdom of God to many who come to swell the ranks of a work of which we are a part, but we are not just as glad about other efforts and conquests that occur anywhere in the Church, our charity is not perfect.

We should approach the persons, circumstances put next to us, by trying to intuit and discover in them and in the groups to which they belong, the task, the mission, the plan God has thought out for them. And to love these brothers of ours in such a way that this programme is realized.

Only if we act like this, with a love that thinks of the good and the increase of other Catholic works like our own, are we worthy apostles, sons of the Church and truly serving it.

If then we ourselves are called to belong to certain institutions that can seem outdated, before thinking of opposing them, or of getting ready for a demanding *aggiornamento*, it will be well worthwhile to place ourselves before God and consider the respect we owe to the Church and to all in its bosom.

It is not Christian to stop only at observing the gaps or in moaning over structures that seem by now emptied of meaning.

We should remember, before everything else, how much suffering these works cost their founders. We should think of the faith, at times more than tested, of the courage and sacrifice of their first companions, of the love which the Church showed towards them at the time, in studying them, supporting them, approving them, encouraging them. We cannot forget their past glory, nor the good, nor the fruits, often great, which they still bear.

These works must be entered 'on tiptoe', as though we were entering a church, with veneration, knowing that our contribution is that of loving them, loving the persons, the aims, the activities, so that we rediscover together the beauty and that something which is always up to date which they cherish, to the consolation of those who form part of it.

Every work has its own function and is, therefore, in some way irreplaceable. The warmth of our love can help it to hear again the echo of the love of God that gave it birth, and it will have the courage to update itself, to increase and multiply.

As the sun cannot but warm, so love cannot but renew, bring new growth and rejuvenate every member and group of the mystical Body, the Church.

HE KNOWS EVERYTHING

JESUS KNOWS EVERYTHING. He reads all our hearts, all our thoughts.

How consoling for us when we lift up to God supplications, or praise or acts of love from the depths of our soul. He hears them, he knows them.

A page of the Gospel tells how he knew every detail about Thomas: from the finger he wanted to put into the nail marks to the hand in his side.

Jesus, God, knows everything.

What a comfort for whoever prays! We are heard, then. This is enough for us. Whether or not the answer is yes is another matter: he knows what is good for us.

Thomas replies with the wonderful words: 'My Lord and my God!', and they are the words that should spontaneously burst out from our heart when we read that passage in the Gospel.

WHOEVER LIVES THE PRESENT

IF SCRIPTURE TEACHES us to do the little things well, this is just the characteristic of someone who does nothing other than what God asks of him in the present moment.

If a person is living in the present, God lives in him and if God is in him, charity is in him. Whoever lives the present is patient, is persevering, is gentle, is poor in all things, is pure, is merciful, because he has love in its highest and most genuine form: he truly loves God with all his heart, all his soul, all his strength; he is inwardly illuminated and guided by the Holy Spirit and so he does not judge, does not think evil, loves his neighbour as himself, has the strength for the evangelical madness of offering the other cheek, of going the second mile ...

He often has the occasion to 'give to Caesar the things that are Caesar's,' because in many moments he will have to live fully his life as a citizen ... and so on.

In a word, he who lives the present is in Christ, Truth.

And this satisfies the soul which always yearns to possess *all* in every instant of its life.

IN THE MAJESTIC frame of creation, one man stands beside another and the saying is true: 'One man is as good as the next.'

We are all men, who are born, who live, and who die.

Even if the spirit of the world leads and has often led in history to one of our fellow men being made a myth, a god, then history itself has dealt justice, reducing him to dust, just like all the others.

We are men beside other men and nothing more, even if we have different tasks.

And it is just this equality between men that calls for a higher reality: it is this people who asks for its leader, its king, its god.

Man, men, have meaning if in life they meet with their Lord and Creator.

Then life is Life for Man. Because in meeting there is an embrace, a fusion, and the creature lives in his Lord and the Lord in his creature.

Then life is Life, and for God it is Life: 'I am Life' said Christ who is God come on earth.

And this is true. And if it is true we must draw the consequences from this so as not to risk making life a tiring pursuit of something that can never be attained.

THE PROTEST OF HEAVEN

OUR TIMES ARE too full of problems: they can be read on the faces of many people that we meet on the street.

'I have a son who doesn't study and won't pass his exam ...' 'My husband works late ...' 'My mother is sick.' 'Will I be able to buy myself that dress?' 'Can't I scrape up enough for a bit of a holiday?'

We run here, we run there. We make calculations. We worry ourselves. All this for ourselves and for those closest to us.

And if our gaze ventures towards other regions and other countries, we see problems that are a lot greater and more acute: hunger, sickness ... the minimum for survival is lacking.

And if we have a little generosity in our heart, we would like to do something for them as well.

Then perhaps we read by chance unusual words which we realize do not come from the earth, nor from the crowd around us that we know so well. These words say: 'Do not be anxious about your life and what you are to eat, nor about your body and how you are to clothe it ... it is the pagans who set their hearts on all these things. Seek first the Kingdom of God ... and all these things will come to you as well.'

It is a mild protest that Heaven makes to earth, that God makes to men and it opens their eyes so that they know they have a Father who thinks of them.

We still have to run, to do things, to work, to be busy, to tire ourselves ... yes, but for another motive: to seek not bread, nor clothes, nor money, but the Kingdom of God in us, which means trying our best to fulfill not our will, but his.

The Gospel says: the rest will be added on. That's just how it comes: unexpectedly. It comes to your home and you say: 'That's providence!' And this is the experience of all consistent Christians.

Then from your own life you understand that if your tiny problems have found an answer, the best solution to the big ones that torment mankind will be to find the most effective way of bringing the world to know and live the Gospel.

So that we would preach it to everyone, we were told: 'Surely life means more than food and the body more than clothes? Consider how the lilies grow in the fields, they do not work, they do not spin; and yet, I tell you, even Solomon in all his splendour was not attired like one of these.'

In these times, especially in the poorer countries, the major emphasis is often placed on social problems and all efforts are dedicated in this direction also as a religious expression of life.

The Gospel tells us to feed the hungry and clothe the naked. But, taken on their own, such actions may not show Christ's message in all its beauty. They may even in some way falsify it because such acts can leave whoever receives them with a complex about being a 'beneficiary', while the Gospel raises men, all men, to the highest level: to the level of being children of God.

The Gospel is all of a piece and it cannot be truly lived and known in part if we do not know it and live it in its entirety.

The principle remedy for the problems, even

worldly material ones, of the poor nations, is and will remain the proclamation of the Gospel.

It is necessary that all men should know Christ, should seek his Kingdom and his justice, then the rest, all the rest, will come to them as well.

VANITY

IF YOU WALK through certain streets of our cities, you have the painful impression that vanity incarnate is walking there. Vanity incarnate in what covers the walls and reveals people in a suffocating immodesty, and in an anti-aesthetic that crushes the heart.

Then, as if attracted by the warmth of a fire in the frostiness of a bitter winter, you take refuge in a church, where the red flame tells you that he is living there.

And there you realize that if it seemed to you that vanity was embodied in the street, the real presence of God which recalls the angels and saints who are already living with him and your dear ones who have passed into the embrace of the Lord, are the true realities in Reality.

In this way the world is made once more the footstool of he who alone 'is', just as hell is the background for Paradise.

THE FASTER THE SPEED

WHEN WE ARE going slowly, as we do when we are walking, we have to use our strength and move ourselves with our legs.

When we ride a bicycle, the bicycle does something for us, and some of our limbs can almost rest.

When a pilot flies a plane and, in this case the speed is very high, his work during the flight is quite limited. The engine does most of the work.

In order to get to the moon, man does very little in comparison with the technical functioning of his space capsule.

The same is true of the soul. The more it moves towards God and gets closer to him, the more it is carried by God. At a certain point, the only thing that is left to do is allow itself to be carried: its effort is directed above all to this.

THESE ARE NOT times noted for penance. On the contrary, it is often criticized as an obscure tradition from the distant past.

Ours is an age in which love leaps into prominence.

Because God is Love.

The starting point of people's conversions today is often that they believe in love. When this happens, a new flow of life springs up. Faith in God's love opens our eyes to see men, things and the various circumstances of life as manifestations of this love and faith in love gives us an explanation of them which is full of light.

It is not difficult then, rather it is almost impossible not to respond to this love, to all it asks, to what it desires, and God's commandments become the means for us to be able to correspond to love with love.

And what is more, the soul unconsciously becomes aware that suffering is something sacred and is not to be rejected but welcomed, even desired. The soul discovers that it is by suffering that God has shown his love to us; and it is by suffering, rununciation, by the death of our self that we can return his love. And the need for penance emerges again from another direction.

We can go on screaming, and overthrow the order of things, we can claim new, absurd and unlawful liberties, and we can open up to a healthy renewal, but as long as we wish to remain Christian, no matter where we turn, there are two things we must recognize. That God is love and that he is crucified love.

AUTHENTICITY

TODAY WE OFTEN hear about Christianity as a social message. And it is only right that this aspect should be emphasized. Since God became man, it is plain that he is concerned with every aspect of our affairs. Christ's whole life is, in fact, an example of social involvement.

It must be remembered, however, that what he announced is also and is above all, a spiritual message.

We Christians do great injustices to our faith.

Now and then we pluck up the courage to love God and our fellow men, to be tolerably good and honest. Not infrequently, we pray. In short, we lead a life that has an undeniably christian flavour.

But there are truths which we neglect, let's admit it, and almost never think about or consider only when we are *forced* to do so.

It happens to me, too, from time to time, and I consider it a real grace, that my eyes open and I become aware of a truth so beautiful that my mind can only barely touch it, because it is not able to grasp the truth: it is too great.

Even so it wakes me up, it shakes me, it encourages me and makes me delighted.

I realize where I am going. I remember that it was announced to me, and I believe with my whole being that if I succeed in performing the duties that God has commanded me, *I shall go ... to Paradise.*

Paradise.

But do we think about this? Do we realize that this is not the place that we should always be improving, making our existence as trouble-free as possible, but that every second of our life is a new step towards another kingdom, another land, towards a homeland where the purest and full happiness we are longing for, will be ours for ever and ever.

And what will be there?

It is better not to risk talking about it. We'll spoil its realities by silly fantasies.

It will be ... it will be ... Paradise!

Today part of society is in protest. Today we have to get rid of masks. The big schemes break down, the 'pseudos' are detected. There is a general demythologizing of everything or everyone regarded as an idol until yesterday.

People demand authenticity, truth.

And if in the course of our history and of the present generation, we let God's providence act, we'll see that what Ladislaus Boros, a contemporary writer has affirmed, has come true.

Having made an acute and blunt, but realistic analysis of the thought and aspirations of men of today, he says: 'Contemporary man cannot call himself modern if he does not encounter Christ.'

This is it: authenticity means truth and the truth is Christ with all he brought, with all he commanded, with what he promised, with the *place* he is preparing for us in *his* kingdom.

This is reality.

But if this is the way things are, what inconsistency there is in our life, what an inversion of values!

We carry on as if it was no longer true that for someone making a long journey to his own

149

dear home, the nearer he gets, the faster his heart beats in him.

Who then is more fortunate and, consequently, happier? The little child or the young person awaiting the often lengthy trial of life, with its joys, yes, but above all with its unfailing sorrows, or the mature adult and, even more, the aged person drawing near the threshold of complete embrace with the love always dimly sought here, and soon to be found there face to face and possessed for ever?

When the first grey hairs appear, when tired limbs cannot be relied on any longer, when age increases and the years add up, how is it that all this, even in us Christians, leads to a feeling of melancholy, of sadness?

We could understand it if we thought that these were the first symptoms of life passing.

But if this is not so, because it is not so, since the greatest adventure for which we appeared one day on this planet still has to begin, how can we justify our reaction? Where has our faith gone?

Have we not got the same attitude as the materialist who only believes in what he can touch and see?

150

'My kingdom is *not* of this world,' Jesus said to Pilate, just because, among other things, he would not fear that Jesus would dethrone him here on earth.

Oh no! There is death, but then there is life, the full life that will never end.

And if a small or even a high price has to be paid to attain it, it is well worth it. In the style of his age, the poor man of Assisi who saw clearly, said: 'So great is the good that awaits me that every pain is a delight for me.'

The chrysalis is ugly while it is being transformed, but afterwards it will be a butterfly.

The same is true of men. We should remember that the more something seems to indicate the end and death, the more it announces life.

This is the pure truth.

Many of us, I think, need to reconvert ourselves, so that we can cheerfully and joyfully spread wisdom and understanding in the world, the fruits of experience.

And when we are also drawing near to our flight and are close to our 'birthday', if we can only repeat the words of the apostle John in his old age, 'Love one another,' we will have said much more and much better than all the great speeches of our lives, when we had youth and strength on our side. And, for mankind who still must wait and journey on, we will have offered the greatest and most shining service.